Paranormal Field Guides

HOW TO FIND WEREWOLVES

Thomas Kingsley Troupe

BLACK
RABBIT
BOOKS

Hi Jinx is published by Black Rabbit Books
P.O. Box 227, Mankato, Minnesota, 56002.
www.blackrabbitbooks.com
Copyright © 2023 Black Rabbit Books

Marysa Storm, editor; Michael Sellner, designer
and photo researcher

Library of Congress Cataloging-in-Publication Data
Names: Troupe, Thomas Kingsley, author.
Title: How to find werewolves / Thomas Kingsley Troupe.
Description: Mankato, Minnesota : Black Rabbit Books, 2023. |
Series: Hi jinx. Paranormal field guides | Includes bibliographical references
and index. | Audience: Ages 8-12 | Audience: Grades 4-6 |
Summary: "With fun facts, a colorful design, and critical thinking questions,
How to Find Werewolves inspires readers to take their love of the paranormal
to the next level all while laughing and learning"– Provided by publisher.
Identifiers: LCCN 2020034524 (print) | LCCN 2020034525 (ebook) |
ISBN 9781623107215 (hardcover) | ISBN 9781644665701 (paperback) |
ISBN 9781623107277 (ebook)
Subjects: LCSH: Werewolves–Juvenile literature.
Classification: LCC GR830.W4 T759 2022 (print) | LCC GR830.W4 (ebook) |
DDC 398.24/54–dc23
LC record available at https://lccn.loc.gov/2020034524
LC ebook record available at https://lccn.loc.gov/2020034525

Image Credits

CONTENTS

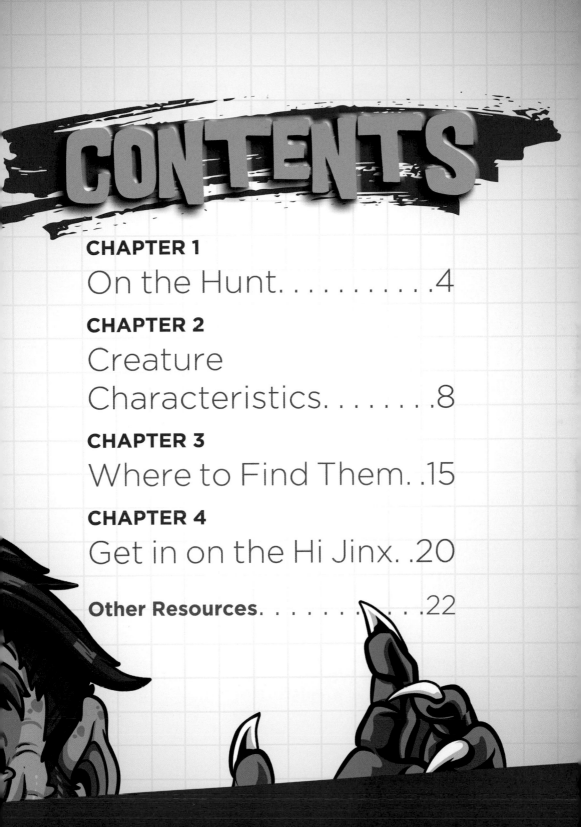

Chapter 1

ON THE HUNT

You really shouldn't be out here! The moon is full. That means werewolves **prowl** the woods. What's that? You actually WANT to find werewolves? I can't believe what I'm hearing! These creatures are monsters. They'll turn you into confetti!

Well, if you're set on finding them, you're in luck. I'm a werewolf expert.* This handy guide will show you how it's done.

*Expert's Note

I was on the cover of *Werewolf Weekly* magazine last August.

Thomas Kingsley Troupe

Thomas Kingsley Troupe is not well-known for his werewolf research. We've never even heard of *Werewolf Weekly*! But he sure loves talking about the monsters. According to him, there's no one better to write this book.

Handy and Helpful

These monsters are very dangerous. They have absolutely terrible breath too. Thankfully, you've got my field guide. You're going to learn a ton about these hairy horrors. So keep this book close while you're werewolf watching.

Stories say a werewolf bite can turn a human into another werewolf.

Chapter 2

CREATURE CHARACTERISTICS

To search for werewolves, you must know what they look like. Werewolves are large and hairy. They have both human and wolf features. Most of them stand up on two legs. They have long **snouts** and big, nasty teeth. Their hands have sharp claws, perfect for ripping **flesh**. Most werewolves don't have tails. If you see a wagging tail, it's probably your neighbor's dog. Leave it alone!

Behaviors

Werewolves are just plain strange. They only come out during a full moon. The full moon causes the change from human to horrible beast. As werewolves, people can't control their actions. The beasts take over. They howl at the moon.*

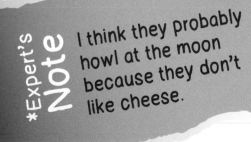

*Expert's Note
I think they probably howl at the moon because they don't like cheese.

Diet

There's a full moon every 29 days. That means werewolves are really hungry. They haven't eaten for almost a month! Now, I hate to say this, but werewolves are bloodthirsty. And that means they'd eat you!

*Expert's Note

Like dogs, werewolves can't have chocolate. Make sure you have vanilla cupcakes.

I actually ran into some werewolves last week. Thankfully, I had some cupcakes with me. I shared them. The werewolves high-fived me before returning to the woods. Sure, werewolves are **carnivores**. But they like treats too.*

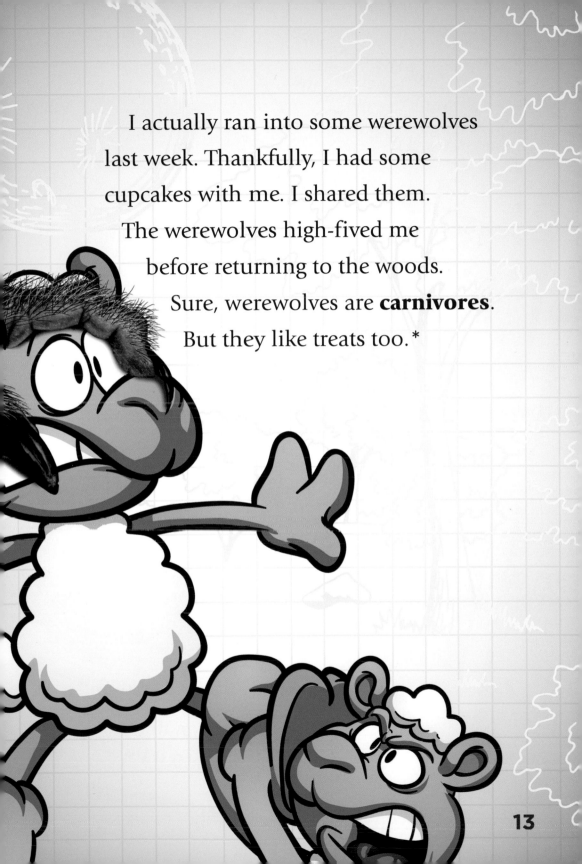

Chapter 3

WHERE TO FIND THEM

People tell werewolf stories around the world. That means these monsters can be found pretty much anywhere. Werewolves like to hunt forests where tasty animals live. It's like a buffet of bunnies, squirrels, and deer.

Sometimes werewolves go to grocery stores. They hang around the **butcher** counter if there's a steak sale. These monsters love a good value.*

Tracking the Creatures

Tracking werewolves isn't hard. They leave all sorts of clues. Look for giant paw prints. Keep your eyes out for fur too. These monsters shed more than a German shepherd!

Since werewolves eat meat, there might be bloody trails to follow. Make sure there are tracks nearby too, though. I followed a blood trail once. It led me to a vampire named Scott.*

*Expert's Note

Vampires and werewolves usually don't get along. If you find a vampire, a werewolf probably isn't nearby.

Now What?

You can't sneak up on a werewolf.
It'll smell you coming miles away.
So the best thing you can do is stay
calm. Maybe toss it a cupcake. Tell the
beast how great its breath smells.*
There's a chance it still might eat you.
But being nice can't hurt.

Either way, you found a werewolf
thanks to me! If you lived long enough
to read this, you're welcome.

*Expert's Note

Only try this if you're
good at acting.

Chapter 4

GET IN ON THE HI JINX

Most people don't believe in werewolves. But you can still look for them if you're feeling brave enough. Try camping with an adult during a full moon. Get permission to explore wooded areas. Visit your library to read stories about werewolves. Search the Internet for photos from fellow hunters. Maybe someday you'll come face-to-face with a real werewolf!

Take It One Step More

1. Pretend you could turn into any sort of creature during a full moon. What would you choose? Why?

2. How do you think werewolf stories started? Research to find out.

3. Imagine your best friend is a werewolf. Would you tell anyone else about their secret? Why or why not?

GLOSSARY

butcher (BOOCH-er)—someone who cuts and sells meat

carnivore (KAR-nuh-vor)—a meat-eating animal

flesh (FLESH)—the soft parts of the body of an animal or person

prowl (PROUL)—to move quietly through an area while hunting

snout (SNOUT)—the projecting part of an animal's face that includes the nose or nose and mouth

BOOKS

Braun, Eric. *How to Outsmart a Werewolf.* How to Outsmart. Mankato, MN: Black Rabbit Books, 2020.

Croy, Anita. *Deadly Beast: A Werewolf Incident.* A Stranger World. Minneapolis: Bearport Publishing Company, 2022.

Troupe, Thomas Kingsley. *Werewolves.* Mythical Creatures. Minneapolis: Bellwether Media, 2021.

WEBSITES

7 Spooky Things You Didn't Know about Werewolves
www.cbc.ca/kidscbc2/the-feed/monsters-101-all-about-werewolves

Totally Crazy Monster Myths (That Are Actually True!)
kids.nationalgeographic.com/explore/monster-myths/

Werewolf Facts for Kids
kids.kiddle.co/Werewolf

INDEX